EXPLORING SCIENCE

KINETIC ENERGY

THE ENERGY OF MOTION

BY DON NARDO

Content Adviser: Steven Shropshire, Ph.D.,
Department of Physics, Idaho State University

Science Adviser: Terrence E. Young Jr., M.Ed., M.L.S.,
Jefferson Parish (Louisiana) Public School System

Reading Adviser: Rosemary G. Palmer, Ph.D., Department of Literacy,
College of Education, Boise State University

 Compass Point Books • Minneapolis, Minnesota

Compass Point Books • 3109 West 50th Street, #115 • Minneapolis, MN 55410

Visit Compass Point Books on the Internet at *www.compasspointbooks.com*
or e-mail your request to *custserv@compasspointbooks.com*

Photographs ©: Corbis/Alan Schein Photography, cover; Peter Arnold/QINETIQ LTD, 4; Shutterstock/Tudor Stanica, 5; Peter Arnold/Yavuz Arslan, 6; Peter Arnold/BIOS Gunther Michel, 8; Peter Arnold/Martin Bond, 10; Peter Arnold/Steven Kazlowski, 11; Shutterstock/Francisco Amaral Leitão, 12; Peter Arnold/Alfred Pasieka, 14; Corbis/Hulton-Deutsch Collection, 16; Peter Arnold/Christoph Busse, 17; Peter Arnold/Keith Ken, 18; Shutterstock/Jarvis Gray, 19; Shutterstock/J. Helgason, 21; Peter Arnold/Patrick Frischknecht, 22; Shutterstock/A.S. Zain, 23; Shutterstock/Eddie Lepp. 24; Corbis/George Hall, 25; Shutterstock/Keith Lamond, 26; Shutterstock/Liv Falvey, 28; Shutterstock/Mikhail Lavrenov, 29; Peter Arnold/Dennis Di Cicco, 30; Reuters/Corbis, 31; Shutterstock/Steve Reed, 33; Shutterstock/Matthew Jacques, 34; Peter Arnold/Clyde H. Smith, 35; Mike Agliolo/Photo Researchers, Inc., 37; Hulton-Deutsch Collection/CORBIS, 38; Photo Researchers, Inc/Publiphoto, 40; Photo Researchers, Inc./D. Van Ravenswaay, 41; Shutterstock/John Kirinic, 42; Zefa/Corbis/Paul C. Pet, 43; Shutterstock/Efras, 44; Shutterstock/Dmitry Kosterev, 46.

Editor: Anthony Wacholtz
Designer: The Design Lab
Page Production: Lori Bye
Photo Researcher: Lori Bye
Illustrators: Ashlee Schultz and Farhana Hossain

Art Director: Jaime Martens
Creative Director: Keith Griffin
Editorial Director: Nick Healy
Managing Editor: Catherine Neitge

Library of Congress Cataloging-in-Publication Data
Nardo, Don, 1947-
Kinetic energy : the energy of motion / by Don Nardo ; illustrators, Ashlee Schultz and Farhana Hossain.
p. cm.—(Exploring science)
ISBN-13: 978-0-7565-3378-6 (library binding)
ISBN-10: 0-7565-3378-3 (library binding)
1. Force and energy—Juvenile literature. 2. Motion—Juvenile literature. 3. Power (Mechanics)—Juvenile literature. I. Schultz, Ashlee, ill. II. Hossain, Farhana, ill. III. Title.

QC73.4.N37 2008
531'.6—dc22   2007004605

About the Author

In addition to his acclaimed volumes on ancient civilizations, historian Don Nardo has published several studies of scientific discoveries and phenomena, as well as scientists. Nardo lives with his wife, Christine, in Massachusetts.

TABLE OF CONTENTS

CHAPTER ONE

The Energy of Motion

THE UNIVERSE AND WORLD we live in are filled with numerous kinds of energy. Among these is light, which allows us to see. There are many types of invisible energy, such as radio waves. These carry music, television images, and cell phone messages from one city or continent to another.

Just as important is kinetic energy, the energy of motion. In many ways, kinetic energy makes nature, the world, and the universe run. If kinetic energy did not exist, everything around us would be motionless and quiet. All matter and objects—both living and non-living—would be unable to move. There would be no sound waves to carry noises to our ears. The entire universe would be incredibly cold because another familiar form of kinetic energy—heat—would be missing, too.

WORK VERSUS THE CAPACITY FOR WORK

Fortunately, we do not live in a cold, dark, or boring universe. Thanks to kinetic energy, we are surrounded by warmth, sounds, and motion. In fact, kinetic energy is a form of motion. Something gains or loses kinetic energy if a force acts on it to

Across Earth's surface, people, animals, and objects are capable of movement because of kinetic energy.

do work. Thus, forces acting to do work make kinetic energy and all forms of motion possible. From speeding race cars and flying birds to howling winds and orbiting planets, all exhibit kinetic energy and happen because of forces that do work.

Kinetic energy is different from potential energy, the other major form of energy. Potential energy is "stored" and has the potential to do work. Only when that potential is unleashed does potential energy convert, or change, into kinetic energy and produce motion.

Race-car driving is a sport built around motion, with cars that can travel more than 200 miles (320 kilometers) an hour.

Consider, for example, a person with a bow and arrow. The archer places the arrow on the bowstring, pulls the bowstring back, and aims at the target. At that moment, there is no movement. The archer's muscles, the bow, and the arrow all contain pent-up potential energy. The instant the archer shoots, the potential energy is converted into kinetic energy. The archer lets go of the string, and the string pushes the arrow toward the target.

The shape of a bow and the elasticity, or flexibility, of the string maximize the force on the arrow once the potential energy is converted to kinetic energy.

A DAY AT THE AMUSEMENT PARK

Another example of potential energy changing into kinetic energy can be seen with a roller coaster. When the car carrying the passengers reaches the top of each towering peak, it slows and levels out. At that moment, most of the energy is potential. Then the car hurtles downward.

Gravity pulls at the mass of the car and its passengers, converting the stored-up energy into a burst of kinetic energy that thrills the riders. During the course of the ride, they will feel repeated energy conversions of this kind.

ENERGY TRANSFORMATIONS

The change from potential energy to kinetic energy is not the only energy conversion that can happen. When an archer fires an arrow, it strikes the target with considerable force and abruptly stops. A small amount of the arrow's kinetic energy converts back into potential energy, but most of it transforms into heat energy. For a few seconds, both the metal arrowhead and the wooden target feel a bit warmer after the impact. Some

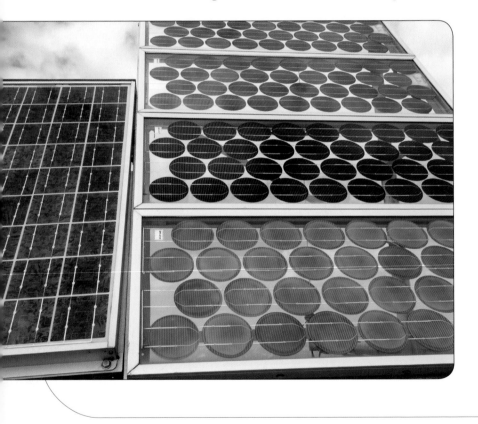

Solar panels absorb energy from the sun and convert it to electrical energy.

of the energy goes into cutting or breaking the target, and some of the arrow's kinetic energy changes into sound energy. The thumping sound of the impact speeds back to the archer's ears. During a roller coaster ride, motion is not the only form of kinetic energy released as the passenger car rushes down an incline. The car's metal wheels grind along the track, producing friction—a force that impedes movement when two surfaces rub against each other. Because of the friction, both the track and wheels grow warmer. Sound energy is also produced in the form of rumbling and screeching noises.

Other transformations from one kind of kinetic energy into another are all around us. Wind energy pushes on sails and makes boats move. Wind also makes the blades of windmills move, producing electrical energy to power homes and businesses. Still another example is what happens in a car engine. Gasoline burns, making various engine parts move. In this way, chemical and heat energy are converted into a kind of motion called mechanical energy.

DID YOU KNOW?

Scientists have learned that energy cannot be created or destroyed. Therefore, no energy is ever lost. This natural principle is called the Law of Conservation of Energy.

ENERGY CHAINS

In some cases, many energy conversions occur in succession, creating an energy chain. The way a coal-burning power station operates is a good example. The station workers burn coal, which contains a great deal of chemical potential energy.

During the burning process, much kinetic energy is produced in the form of heat. That energy is used to heat water, making steam. In turn, the steam causes big circular shafts called turbines to spin, thereby generating mechanical energy. Next, a device called a generator converts this mechanical energy into electrical energy. Finally, household lamps, radios, and furnaces transform the electrical energy into light, sound, and heat.

A coal-burning power plant converts the chemical energy created from burning coal into many other forms of energy, a process that eventually produces electricity.

CHAPTER TWO

Kinetic Energy and Atoms

WHEN PEOPLE HEAR the word *motion*, they usually think about familiar moving objects, such as people walking, basketballs bouncing, or airplanes flying. All of these things possess kinetic energy.

There are more basic examples of kinetic energy in nature, however. Kinetic energy actually begins with atoms, the building blocks of all matter. This world is microscopic and invisible to the human eye because atoms are extremely tiny. If you could line up 250 million atoms in a row, they would measure just 1 inch (2.5 centimeters) in length.

Because atoms are so small, we cannot sense the movements of a single atom. Even thousands or tens of thousands of atoms in motion would be hard to detect. But we can feel the combined movements of millions, billions, and trillions of atoms. Two major effects of their movements, or kinetic energy, are heat and electricity.

Kinetic energy is present even in the smallest of movements, such as a bird opening its beak to chirp.

VIBRATING MOLECULES

Heat is the result of trillions of moving atoms and molecules, which are tiny clusters of atoms. Almost every substance in nature is composed of molecules. One of the more familiar molecules—a water molecule—is made up of one oxygen atom and two hydrogen atoms. A single drop of water contains billions upon billions of water molecules.

The way water molecules behave shows how kinetic energy produces heat. The slower the molecules move, the less heat they have. Slower-moving water molecules tend to stick together and form ice. If these molecules moved slowly enough, they would reach the lowest temperature possible: minus 460 degrees Fahrenheit (minus 273 degrees Celsius). Scientists call it absolute zero.

The rapid movement of molecules in a fire produces heat energy.

Temperature, which is a measurement of heat, is a product of the kinetic energy of molecules. The faster water molecules move, the higher the temperature they achieve. As the temperature rises, ice begins to melt into water. If the kinetic energy of the molecules increases, the molecules vibrate wildly. No longer able to stick together, they float into the air as steam, a kind of gas. In this way, heat energy can cause any substance to change its state of matter.

STATES OF MATTER

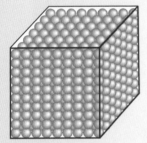

Solid
An ice cube is made up of water molecules that are packed closely and bound to each other. In this form, water has a definite shape.

Liquid
When ice is heated, it becomes a liquid. The water then takes the shape of the container it is in. The water molecules are not bound together, and they move around each other.

Gas
When even more heat is added to the water, the molecules move apart even more and move freely in all directions. As a gas, it is known as steam.

HEAT FLOW

Water is not the only substance that kinetic energy can change from a solid to a gas. At high enough temperatures, any form of matter can become a gas. If still more energy is added to a gas, the molecules will have so much energy that their vibrations rip each molecule apart to form smaller particles. What used to be a gas then becomes plasma. This is what happens inside stars like the sun. At temperatures of more than tens of thousands of degrees, even metals exist as plasma.

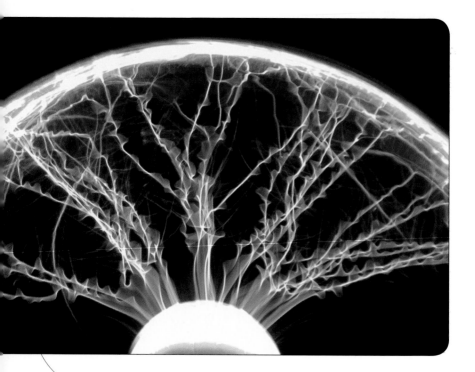

In a plasma globe, strands of plasma are created from the motion of electrons and other particles. These strands are drawn to a person's fingertips if they are near the globe.

DID YOU KNOW?

Heat will flow from cooler objects to warmer objects if enough work is performed. This is how refrigerators, heat pumps, and air conditioners work.

Given enough time, hot things—including stars—tend to cool off because of a process called heat flow. Unless they are stimulated to move faster, atoms and molecules tend to slow down over time. As their kinetic energy decreases, so does the temperature of the substance they make up. On its own, heat flow always moves energy from higher temperatures to lower ones. Imagine a person jumping or falling into freezing water. The water is much colder than the person's body, so the body heat rapidly flows outward into the cold water. If the person stays in the water too long, he or she will freeze to death.

ELECTRICAL KINETIC ENERGY

Atoms and molecules are not the only things that produce kinetic energy on the atomic level. Each atom is made up of even tinier particles—protons, neutrons, and electrons—called subatomic particles. Protons and neutrons make up the nucleus, or center, of an atom. Electrons are much smaller and orbit the nucleus.

Measuring Energy

In 1845, English scientist James Joule discovered that heat is a form of energy. He placed a small paddle wheel in some water and attached a weight suspended by a pulley. Each time the weight dropped and turned the wheel (a form of work), the temperature of the water rose slightly. Joule found that the same amount of work always produced the same amount of heat. He calculated standard units for measuring heat and named them joules, after himself. A thousand joules make up a kilojoule.

Experiments performed by James Joule (1818–1889) proved that heat is produced by motion.

Under certain conditions, some of an atom's electrons can break free and move on their own. Each electron carries a negative electrical charge. When billions or trillions of electrons flow together, it is called electricity.

Today the most familiar kind of electricity powers homes, stores, and other buildings. Flows of electrons are channeled through metal wires. The resulting electrical current can be controlled using switches.

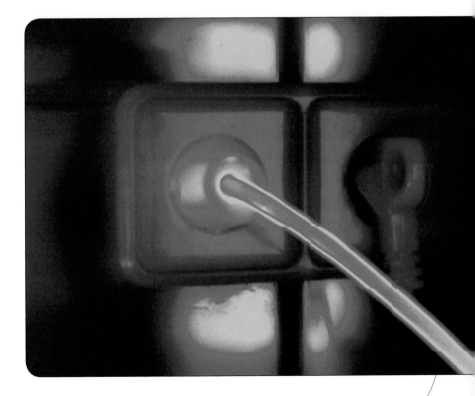

Thermal imagery allows us to see the concentration of heat in an electrical wire leading to an outlet.

Electrical kinetic energy also exists in a number of natural, uncontrolled situations. The most visible, spectacular, and dangerous is lightning. You can experiment with a safer version of electrical energy using a simple comb. Run the comb through your hair several times. Then hold the comb an inch or two above your head. Some of the hairs will rise toward the comb. Some of the electrons in the hairs' atoms rubbed off, giving the comb a negative electrical charge and leaving some atoms in the hair with a positive charge. Because positive and negative charges attract each other, the hairs (+) are drawn toward the comb (-).

Lightning bolts can reach 50,000 degrees Fahrenheit (27,760 degrees Celsius), which is five times hotter than the sun.

Energy and Waves ⊕

EVERYONE HAS SEEN WAVES moving through liquids, especially water. Waves can form in any amount of water. In a bathtub, they are small, while waves in a pond can be much larger.

Waves are another example of energy in action. A wave, more properly called a mechanical wave, is a burst of energy moving through a substance. That substance—which can be a solid, liquid, gas, or plasma—is called a medium.

Some of the largest waves are found in oceans.

WAVES

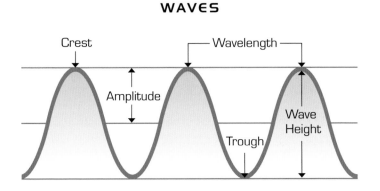

Crest — Wavelength — Amplitude — Trough — Wave Height

Each wave has a high point and a low point. The wave's high point is called the crest, and the low point is called the trough. The distance from the top of one crest to the top of the next crest is called the wavelength. The wavelength can also be measured between two troughs. Half of the vertical distance between a trough and the next crest is called the amplitude. The wavelength of a group of waves can reveal the amount of energy in the waves. Suppose you visit the same beach two days in a row. On the first day, the waves are long and lazy, with crests spaced 60 feet (18.3 meters) apart. On the second day, the height, or amplitude, of the waves is about the same, but the wavelength is only 10 feet (3.1 m). Therefore, six waves now exist in the space occupied by a single wave the day before.

The shorter waves from day two are more energetic. That is because there is more motion, and thus more kinetic energy passes through the water on the second day. As the wave moves along, water molecules push on other water molecules. In turn, these push on still more molecules, transferring the wave and the energy it carries through the water.

Because the waves on day two are more frequent, they are said to have a higher frequency. A wave's frequency is the number of wavelengths, or wave crests, that pass by a fixed point each second.

Waves with lower frequencies, such as calm waves in an ocean, are long and slow. Waves with higher frequencies are short and energetic.

CAUSES OF OCEAN WAVES

The frequency and strength of waves is partly determined by the event that produces them. Most ocean waves are caused by wind blowing across the water's surface. The stronger the wind, the bigger and stronger the waves it will produce.

Sometimes ocean waves are set in motion by disturbances such as earthquakes or landslides. These violent events release a large amount of kinetic energy. The energy spreads outward in all directions, creating a series of large, powerful waves. The largest are called tsunamis, a Japanese word meaning "harbor waves." Tsunamis can be extremely dangerous and destructive. In December 2004, a tsunami in the Indian Ocean killed more than 200,000 people.

Surface waves in the ocean are created by gusts of wind. The strength of the wind determines the size of the waves.

Walls of Water

The 2004 Indian Ocean tsunami was caused by an enormous earthquake. As a giant chunk of the ocean floor cracked and shifted, huge amounts of kinetic energy were released. The disturbance caused a large tsunami to move outward in all directions. Walls of water rushed ashore in Indonesia, Thailand, Sri Lanka, India, and the Maldives. The wavelength of the tsunami was very long. So as the water made its way toward land, it did not simply break and stop near the shore, as ordinary ocean waves with shorter wavelengths do. Instead, it kept moving inland for thousands of feet until the entire length of the wave had come ashore. In the process, many towns were demolished and thousands of people drowned or were crushed to death.

A tsunami's forceful waves crushed and mangled thousands of homes in Indonesia.

SOUND WAVES

Ocean waves travel at speeds ranging from a few miles per hour to several hundred miles per hour. In contrast, sound waves move faster than water waves, traveling through the air at about 750 miles (1,200 km) per hour, called the "speed of sound."

Like ocean waves, sound waves are generated by disturbances in the medium, in this case the air. Examples of disturbances in the air include a clap of thunder, a dog's bark, and the beat of a drum. Each produces a burst of kinetic and potential energy that ripples through the air. When the waves

When a musician taps on a bongo, air molecules around the bongo head move together and push apart with each vibration. This sends out waves of compressed and expanded molecules. The energy from the waves carries sound to our ears.

enter our ears, they vibrate against our eardrums and produce sounds. The loudness of a sound is determined by the amplitude of the sound wave. Loud sounds have big amplitudes, while soft sounds have small amplitudes.

Sound waves follow the same rules as other waves. Sound waves with tall crests (large amplitudes) and higher frequencies are more energetic and have a higher pitch. Sound waves with lower frequencies and the same amplitude are less forceful. They have a more mellow sound and have a lower pitch.

One of the most spectacular examples of energy and sound waves is a sonic boom. When a jet aircraft flies, it disturbs the air, creating pressure waves. These are similar to the waves that bounce off a ship's bow as the ship moves through the water. As the jet nears the speed of sound, the waves crowd closer and closer together. When the jet exceeds the speed of sound, the waves combine into a powerful wave called a shock wave. A sonic boom is the thunderlike sound created by a shock wave.

A cloud of vapor formed by a shock wave surrounds a jet as it breaks the sound barrier.

CHAPTER FOUR

Energy and Light

THANKS TO THE ENERGY of sound waves, we can hear human speech, music, birds chirping, and other sounds. Another kind of energy—light—allows us to see. Light comes from a variety of sources, some natural and others human-made. Natural sources of light include the sun, lightning, and fire. Human-made sources include light-bulbs, flashlights, car head-lights, and television and computer screens.

THE COLORS OF THE SPECTRUM

Like sound, light moves in waves. That means that it has wavelengths and frequencies as well. A beam of light from the sun contains many different wavelengths. The brightest and most common light from our sun has wavelengths in the visible range, with each representing a different color.

A lightbulb gives off light because of electricity. Electric current flows through the filament, or thin wire, in the lightbulb. As the filament grows warm, it gives off light.

The major colors are always arranged in the same order, by wavelength: red, orange, yellow, green, blue, and violet. Of these, violet light has the shortest wavelengths—about 380 nanometers (nm) to 450 nm. Because the wavelengths of light are extremely tiny, scientists use the nanometer to measure them. Red light has the longest wavelengths—about 620 to 750 nm.

Colors of different wavelengths make up the spectrum of visible light. They can be seen in a rainbow following a thunderstorm or in a fine spray from a garden hose. Mixed together, the colors of the spectrum combine into ordinary white light. This can be tested in a simple experiment. First, use a pencil or pen to create three pie slices of the same size on a circular piece of paper. Then paint one pie slice red, another

VISIBLE SPECTRUM

Visible light is made up of different colors, each with a different frequency.

Color

| Violet | Blue | Green | Yellow | Orange | Red |

Frequency

Highest ·· Lowest

slice blue, and the last slice yellow. Then attach the paper to a toy top and spin the top on a flat surface. If the paper spins fast enough, the colors will merge into an off-white, grayish color.

INCREDIBLY FAST

Although light moves in waves, it behaves as if it were made up of tiny particles. Scientists call these particles photons. Each photon can be described as a tiny packet of energy. Photons of light race along at nature's highest possible speed—about 186,000 miles (300,000 km) per second.

To understand how fast light moves, imagine you are holding an extremely bright flashlight. Beside you stands a large mirror that faces a second mirror 3,000 miles (4,800 km) away (the distance between Los Angeles and New York City). At a given signal, you turn

Following a storm, tiny droplets of water remain in the air. Light from the sun, which has all the colors of the spectrum, turns the droplets into various colors depending on the angle at which the light hits them. The result is a rainbow that arches through the sky.

on the flashlight, and the beam rushes to the second mirror. It bounces off the distant mirror, returns to your mirror, and bounces off again. The light beam continues to race back and forth. In a single second, it crosses a distance as wide as the United States 62 times.

In addition to moving extremely fast, light energy moves independently of physical matter. Sound waves require a medium—most often air—to carry them along. Since there is

Rays of light from the sun travel in straight lines.

no air in outer space, sound cannot travel from Earth to the moon. In contrast, photons of light can travel through a vacuum, an area containing no atoms or molecules. This allows us to see the sun, planets, and other distant heavenly bodies.

We can see the Milky Way galaxy from Earth because light can travel through a vacuum in space.

Seeing into the Past

In a way, energy allows us to see into the past. At light speed, a person could travel around the world seven times in a single second or travel to the moon in less than two seconds. However, the universe is so immense that even light takes a long time to cross it.

Proxima Centauri, the nearest star besides the sun, is 4.2 light-years away. That means light coming from that star takes 4.2 years to reach Earth. If you were to look at Proxima Centauri tonight, you would see it as it looked 4.2 years ago. Moreover, if it blew up tonight, we would not know it. We would continue to see the star shining in the sky until the light from the explosion reached us 4.2 years from now.

NASA's Hubble Space Telescope captured a picture of the remnants of a star that exploded thousands of years ago.

BEYOND HUMAN VISION

Visible light is not the only form of energy that travels through space at light speed. Scientists recognize several types of fast-moving energy, collectively known as electromagnetic radiation. Visible light consists of electromagnetic wavelengths visible to human eyes. Beyond the range of human vision lie infrared light, ultraviolet light, and other kinds of electromagnetic radiation.

ELECTROMAGNETIC SPECTRUM

The electromagnetic spectrum includes the complete range of radiant energy, from the longest radio waves to the shortest gamma rays.

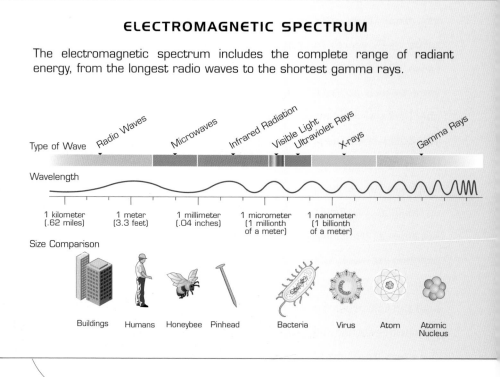

Radio waves are a familiar form of invisible energy. Stars, including the sun, regularly give off radio waves. Huge explosions of hot gases on the sun unleash bursts of radio waves that instruments on Earth detect and measure. Various human-made electronic devices also emit and collect radio waves. These streams of radiation carry voices, music, and images to radios and televisions.

Another familiar form of electromagnetic radiation—an X-ray—is more energetic than either visible light or radio waves. Stars and other cosmic bodies give off X-rays. But this type of radiation is better known for its use in medicine. In an X-ray machine, a beam of X-rays passes through the body and strikes a photographic plate. This produces a ghostly image of the patient's insides. Televisions and X-ray machines are examples of people putting nature's energy to work for humanity's benefit.

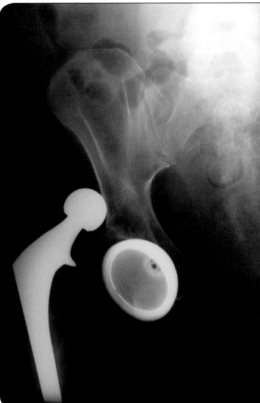

X-rays allow doctors to see the inside the human body to find any problems, such as a replacement hip that has become dislocated.

CHAPTER FIVE

Energy and Global Catastrophes

KINETIC ENERGY is all around us. In some cases, its effects can easily be seen, such as with moving animals, cars, planets, and ocean waves. In other cases—including sound waves, plumes of heat, and pulses of radio waves and X-rays—energy is invisible.

Whether visible or invisible, energy can cause constant change. Most of the time, that change is gradual. For example, ocean waves, wind, and sunlight change the shape of beaches and coastlines through erosion. Slowly changing patterns of weather and plant growth can affect the lives of animal species. Over the course of hundreds and thousands of years, these changes make some animals more successful, while others become less successful. Some steadily dwindle in numbers and become extinct.

Every now and then, a great deal of energy is unleashed in a short time span. This can cause sudden

Over time, water erosion smooths the surfaces of rocks.

and often disastrous changes in weather patterns, plant growth, and animal life. The result is a global catastrophe that abruptly alters the course of history.

No large-scale global catastrophes have occurred in the relatively short time that human civilizations have existed on Earth. But evidence has been found for many such disasters

Violent volcanic eruptions may have caused worldwide devastation millions of years ago.

in past ages. A few of the catastrophes happened when objects from outer space struck the planet. Some of these extra-terrestrial visitors were asteroids, hunks of rock or rock mixed with iron and other metals. Others were comets, cosmic objects made up of rock and ice.

AN ENORMOUS FIREBALL

Around 65 million years ago, dinosaurs were the most dominant creatures on Earth. According to some scientists, an asteroid or comet approached the planet one day. Scientists estimate that it was about 6 miles (9.6 km) across and trav-eled between 12 and 42 miles (19.2 and 67.2 km) per second. The bigger an object is, the more potential energy it possesses. Also, faster-moving objects have more kinetic energy than slower-moving ones. Therefore, the asteroid or comet had a vast quantity of stored-up energy. It was equivalent to the energy of five billion atomic bombs.

At a spot above the Yucatan Peninsula, in what is now

DID YOU KNOW?

The cosmic impact that occurred 65 million years ago created a huge explosion equal to about 100 trillion tons of dynamite—enough to fill millions of train cars—exploding all at once.

eastern Mexico, the speeding rock exploded. In an instant, the potential energy stored inside the object was converted into kinetic and light energy. Some of that energy took the form of extreme heat, and an enormous fireball spread outward in all directions. Other stored-up energy converted into shock

A massive asteroid or comet may have collided with Earth when the dinosuars ruled the planet.

waves in the atmosphere that plunged through the air with the power of a giant hammer. These waves flattened every tree and destroyed every animal within a thousand miles of the impact.

Meanwhile, more kinetic energy was released as shock waves in the ground. Gigantic earthquakes, hundreds of times more violent than any ever experienced by humans, rocked the continents. The shaking dislodged part of the seafloor

A shock wave emerges from the base of a tremendous impact, such as a nuclear explosion.

near Mexico. This sent another wave of kinetic energy outward in the form of a tsunami. In the next day or two, monstrous waves battered all of the world's coastlines.

CHAIN REACTION OF DEATH

In the hours and days following the great impact, the kinetic energy it unleashed took on other deadly forms. The blast broke away large amounts of rock, dust, and other debris from the ground, which flew upward and outward at hundreds of miles per hour. Billions of chunks flew high into the atmosphere, and a few kept on going into space. However, most of them eventually came back down again. As they did, they smashed into air molecules. This converted some of the kinetic energy of the falling material into heat energy. The result was a rain of fiery debris that set all the forests in the world ablaze.

These global fires sent millions of tons of smoke and soot skyward. Soon skies across the planet grew dark and remained dark for a long time. Without sunlight, most of the plants that had survived the fires died. Dinosaurs and other animals that ate plants could not sustain themselves. Meat eaters, which ate the plant eaters, also lost their main food source and died.

After a few years, Earth's atmosphere and weather returned to normal, but the world was now a very different place. All

of the dinosaurs were gone. Up to 70 percent of the planet's animals and plants had disappeared. Some of the creatures that hid in underground burrows survived. Among these were primitive mammals. Some scientists believe that all of the diverse mammals that exist today, including humans, developed from these disaster survivors.

The impact of a large asteroid or comet is one of the two main theories explaining how the dinosaurs died 65 million

The aftereffects of the asteroid or comet collision may have caused the dinosaurs to become extinct.

The Devil's Tail

The disaster that may have wiped out the dinosaurs left a large scar on Earth's surface. The explosion carved out a crater about 185 miles (300 km) across on the Yucatan Peninsula, in eastern Mexico. Its existence was confirmed in 1991 by scientists from NASA's Ames Research Center. They found that part of the crater lies beneath the land, while the rest is buried in the nearby seabed. Over time, weather and other natural forces partially erased the crater. Today most of it is very hard to see.

At first the researchers were unsure whether this was the crater from the blast that may have killed the dinosaurs. Scientists performed tests on the rocks in the area, which dated the crater's formation to 65 million years ago, exactly when the disaster occurred. The scientists named the crater Chicxulub, a word meaning "tail of the devil" in the Mayan language.

years ago. The other major theory also involves an immense outburst of energy. Evidence shows that several large volcanoes erupted with extreme violence for a long time. Gigantic amounts of heat energy, poisonous gases, and soot killed many plant and animal species. Some scientists think that the asteroid impact and super-volcanic event occurred around the same time. If so, the double disaster ensured that few living things would survive.

Fossils are all that remain of the dinosaurs.

Other global disasters of various sizes have happened before, and scientists say that others will occur in the future. There is no way to know when a similar catastrophe will happen, but one thing is certain: Nature has the power to unleash enormous amounts of energy, either a little at a time or all at once.

Major volcanoes covered Earth with ash, fire, soot, and poisonous gases millions of years ago.

In the meantime, human beings everywhere continue to experience lives that are dependent on a wide range of energy forms. From the sounds we hear to the heat that warms our skin, we are completely surrounded by energy. Thanks to kinetic energy, we walk, work, jump, swim, and ride in a wide variety of sights and sounds.

Kinetic energy makes the world an interesting and exciting place to live.

conversion—in science, the process of changing one form of
energy into another

electricity (or electrical energy)—flow or stream of charged
particles, such as electrons

electromagnetic radiation—light, radio waves, microwaves,
X-rays, and other energetic forms of energy that travel at the
speed of light

frequency—the rate at which an event occurs; for example, the
number of wavelengths, or wave crests, that pass by a fixed
point each second

friction—force that occurs when two surfaces rub against
each other, partially impeding movement

heat flow—natural flow of energy from higher temperatures
to lower ones

kinetic energy—energy, or work, that can be transferred by a
moving object

nanometer—one billionth of a meter

photons—particles or units of light or other electromagnetic
radiation

potential energy—energy stored within an object and waiting
to be released

spectrum—rainbow effect that results from the breakdown of
white light

wavelength—distance from one wave crest to the next

▸ The large amounts of kinetic energy given off by stars such as the sun are created in nuclear reactions. These occur in the star's central region. Atoms of hydrogen fuse, or combine, to make atoms of a slightly heavier element—helium. In the process, energy is released in the form of light and other kinds of electromagnetic radiation and heat. Over time, however, the stars cool. Billions of years from now, the sun will become a much smaller and cooler star.

▸ The way sound waves form is illustrated by a musician striking a kettle drum. When the mallet hits the drum, the drum's flexible surface vibrates. Each upward vibration compresses, or bunches together, the air molecules floating above. Each downward vibration draws the molecules apart. These bands of many and few molecules become the crests and troughs of successive sound waves.

▸ Scientists have concluded that light does not have mass. However, it often acts as if it does. The famous German scientist Albert Einstein suggested that the gravity of a large object such as the sun will cause a nearby beam of light to bend slightly. Other scientists confirmed this in 1919. During a solar eclipse, they observed light from a distant star bending toward the sun in the exact manner Einstein had predicted.

A solar eclipse occurs when the moon crosses between Earth and the sun, blocking much of the sun's light from reaching the planet.

At the Library

Bowden, Rob. *Energy.* San Diego: Kidhaven Press, 2003.

Parker, Steve. *Science of Sound: Projects With Experiments With Music and Sound Waves.* Chicago: Heinemann Library, 2005.

Searle, Bobbi. *Heat and Energy.* Brookfield, Conn.: Copper Beach Books, 2001.

Tocci, Salvatore. *Experiments With Energy.* New York: Children's Press, 2003.

On the Web

For more information on this topic, use FactHound.
1. Go to *www.facthound.com*
2. Type in this book ID: 0756533783
3. Click on the *Fetch It* button.
FactHound will find the best Web sites for you.

On the Road

Boston Museum of Science
Science Park
Boston, MA 02114
617/723-2500

Pacific Tsunami Museum
130 Kamehameha Ave.
Hilo, HI 96720
808/935/0926

Explore all the Physical Science books

Atoms & Molecules: Building Blocks of the Universe

Chemical Change: From Fireworks to Rust

Electrical Circuits: Harnessing Electricity

Force and Motion: Laws of Movement

Kinetic Energy: The Energy of Motion

Manipulating Light: Reflection, Refraction, and Absorption

The Periodic Table: Mapping the Elements

Physical Change: Reshaping Matter

Waves: Energy on the Move

A complete list of Exploring Science titles is available on our Web site: *www.compasspointbooks.com*